Lee Hooper

A Critical Examination Between Two Methods in Educational Research: Action Research & Ethnography

Qualitative Research

GRIN Verlag

Bibliografische Information der Deutschen Nationalbibliothek:

Die Deutsche Bibliothek verzeichnet diese Publikation in der Deutschen National-
bibliografie; detaillierte bibliografische Daten sind im Internet über http://dnb.d-
nb.de/ abrufbar.

Imprint:

Copyright © 2013 GRIN Verlag GmbH
Druck und Bindung: Books on Demand GmbH, Norderstedt Germany
ISBN: 978-3-656-51268-4

This book at GRIN:

http://www.grin.com/en/e-book/262264/a-critical-examination-between-two-
methods-in-educational-research-action

GRIN - Your knowledge has value

Der GRIN Verlag publiziert seit 1998 wissenschaftliche Arbeiten von Studenten, Hochschullehrern und anderen Akademikern als eBook und gedrucktes Buch. Die Verlagswebsite www.grin.com ist die ideale Plattform zur Veröffentlichung von Hausarbeiten, Abschlussarbeiten, wissenschaftlichen Aufsätzen, Dissertationen und Fachbüchern.

Visit us on the internet:

http://www.grin.com/

http://www.facebook.com/grincom

http://www.twitter.com/grin_com

267.783 – Assignment 1 (Topic 2)

Qualitative Research: A Critical Examination Between Two Methods in Educational Research – Action Research & Ethnography

Approximate length – 3000 words

Submitted on 16th April, 2013

Action Research – Introduction & Definition

Action Research (AR) is a term used to denote a methodical system of investigation and reflection, performed by individuals for their own professional practice and development (Costello, 2011, pp. 6-7). It encompasses a social philosophy that is centered on acquiring practical knowledge that can be applied to concrete situations (Punch, 2009, p. 136). The goals of AR can be generalized into three potential outcomes: "Improving practice, improving understanding of practice, and improving the situation in which the practice takes place" (Atkins & Wallace, 2012, pp. 126-127).

Key Concepts & Distinctive Features

AR is defined as a cyclical process, with each new piece of information generating new ideas and new questions (Punch, 2009, p. 136-7). There are numerous variations to illustrate the logical steps used in AR, with many including combinations of circles or spirals (Costello, 2011, p. 8). Kemmis and McTaggart (2000, p. 595-596) describe AR as first preparing for an adjustment, then once initiated, observing the results with a reflective attitude. Once this is done the cycle is repeated with the incorporated knowledge of the previous change made. Bassey (1998, pp. 94-95) outlines a more sophisticated eight stage model, revolving around three central themes: exploring the educational environment (Stage 1-4); implementing changes (Stage 5); observing and analysing the changes (Stage 6-8). Costello (2011) summarizes this process stage by stage below:

Stage 1: Defining the enquiry.

Stage 2: Describing the educational situation.

Stage 3: Collecting and analysing evaluative data.

Stage 4: Reviewing the data and looking for contradictions.

Stage 5: Tackling a contradiction by introducing some aspect of change.

Stage 6: Monitoring the change.

Stage 7: Analysing evaluative data concerning the change.

Stage 8: Reviewing the change and deciding what to do next. (p. 10)

AR can be divided into three specific approaches: Practical AR, critical AR, and participatory AR. Practical AR entails devising pedagogical methods in applied settings that directly benefit both teacher and student (Manfra, 2009, p. 32). Critical AR focuses on the examination of social and political influences on the educational environment, so that underlying issues of inequality may be addressed and resolved. Participatory AR is centered on collaborating with participants as equals or colleagues, so that the group can form contextual approaches to increase localized knowledge that can be put into action (Whyte, 1989, pp. 368-369).

Role of the Researcher

Cohen, Manion & Morrison (2007, p. 303) point out that there are two generalized camps in AR: that of the reflective practitioner, who seek to affect change on the micro-level, such as the classroom, and that of the critical theorist, who look towards implementing change on a macro-level, such as changing national school policies. Depending on where in this spectrum the researcher sits, their roles will differ, however, regardless of their position, both researchers will generally be looking to empower those that they are researching.

Those involved in AR are typically not outsiders attempting to gain access to educational matters, but rather insiders who are in some way accountable for what goes on within the educational environment (Sheehy, 2005, p. 205). As insiders who have access to a wider range of connections, there is a heavy emphasis on collaboration. One role of the researcher will be to share information with teachers, students, and other researchers (Cohen et al, 2007, p. 299). The significance of collaborating is that by involving those around who may be on the periphery of your practice, either affecting it directly or indirectly, a more holistic and permanent change is likely to occur. Furthermore, by involving others in this way, AR will likely have a more emancipatory result.

Main Data Collecting Techniques

In AR there is an eclectic approach to collecting raw data, with techniques ranging from a field journal, collecting electronic materials, using sources such as class records, analytic memos or repertory grids, to standard collecting techniques such as questionnaires, surveys, and interviews (Craig, 2009, p. 138; Waters-Adam, 2006, Part 1, Methods, para. 4). One of the defining characteristics about AR is that there is a constant analysis of data throughout the research, which restructures the direction of the study and consequent analysis of further data (Mertler, 2006, p. 28). As a result of this continual examination, the researcher needs to have a structured and logical approach to continual data analysis, since each cycle depends on the analysis and completion of the previous cycle (Atkins & Wallace, 2012, p. 139). In order to identify and note the most relevant information, the researcher may use inductive analysis, where "important patterns and themes are ordered to construct some sort of framework" (Mertler, 2006, p. 125). This can be done through a three step process of "organization, description, and interpretation", which will involve some sort of coding scheme to categorize information in a more manageable way (Parsons & Brown, 2002).

Another method to structure and understand the information is to use a dialectical approach, which identifies the harmonious and contradictory elements of their practice (Waters-Adam, 2006, Part 3, Analysis, para. 1-5). Applying dialectics helps to understand the relationship between the various elements involved and can bring clarity when two actions or ideas are in contradiction (Motley-Abbot, 2006, pp. 37-38). Through observing these contractions a synthesis of action or theory can be made, and then applied to the next problem. This mode of reflection and action in dialectics is akin the cyclical process in AR.

Critical Analysis

One of the strengths of AR is through educators conducting their own research and developing more awareness of classroom issues, areas of interest, self-reflection, and bridging theoretical gaps with practical applications (Cohen et al, 2007, p. 299). The significance of this is that, rather than knowledge or learning being situated in the academic sphere, it transverses into the professional one, which will have greater impact on the development of better educational environments. AR also fosters "self-critical communities" that have the capability to cause change on both social and political levels, and since this process is based on collective sharing, learning, and growing, it has the potential to start or affect social movements (Cohen et al, 2007, p .300).

As for the weaknesses, there are several criticisms of utilizing the AR approach (Waters-Adam, 2006, Part 4, para. 1-5). Firstly, since researchers are typically already involved in their own teaching practice, managing time between research and classroom activities may pose a problem. Secondly, those who are conducting the studies have vested interests in creating change. This could create unintentional bias in the study, as neutrality is harder to maintain. Thirdly, since those who are conducting the study may not have a background in research, there may be issues with the reliability of data collection and analysis, as the researcher may not be familiar with typical methodologies being used. Finally, AR is a process where the participation of colleagues, parents, and students is encouraged, and thus open communication is vital (Zeni, 2005, pp. 206-212). Because of this, there are potential confidentiality issues involved and access to certain information must be safeguarded, alongside ownership of academic ideas and responsibility to the participants involved.

Ethnography – Introduction & Definition

Ethnography is based on the understanding that culture plays an integral part within the function and expression of society (Punch, 2009, p. 126). Culture is deemed as the collective ideas, beliefs, and perceptions in a society, which are reflected in the actions and behaviours of those inside the various communities that make up society (Haviland, Prins, McBride, & Walrath, 2011, p. 28). These characteristics are either actively learned or passively shared, and are integrated as functioning parts of the society (Eller, 2009, p. 32). By applying an anthropological stance towards ethnography in education, a greater understanding of holistic factors is gained (Spindler & Hammond, 2006, p. XIX). These include acquiring awareness of the origins and justifications of knowledge, power structures, cultural issues, gender roles, and the general attitude of both teachers and students towards education.

Key Concepts & Distinctive Features

The use of fieldwork is considered to be a fundamental part of ethnographic research, with different methodologies being utilised depending on one's theoretical stance and intended goals (Punch, 2009, p.125). The researcher attempts to insert themselves into the daily life of those being studied so that information may be gathered on the 'natural' state of conditions. Punch (2009, pp. 127-128) outlines six distinctive characteristics of ethnography in education:

4

1) The fundamental premise of ethnography is to identify the "meaning of cultural interpretation" within the group (p. 127). That is, becoming aware of the shared and common belief systems, alongside the perceptual patterns associated with these beliefs.

2) It is necessary to gain an insider's perspective on the "meanings that behaviours, actions, events, and contexts have" (p. 127). This means understanding what goes on in the educational environment from the viewpoint of those involved, rather than from those 'outside' of the arena.

3) The research must take place in a natural setting, as modifying or recreating an environment will negatively impact accurate study results.

4) The ethnographer must be flexible as research is an *"unfolding and evolving sort of study,* rather than prestructured" (p. 127).

5) Data collection is focused around fieldwork. A range of eclectic techniques should be utilised in order to achieve the most beneficial results.

6) "Ethnographic *data collection* will typically be *prolonged and repetitive"*, so that information can be verified and recorded in systematic and accurate way (p. 128).

These characteristics then form the basis for a multitude of different ethnographic approaches that can be used. Two methods prevalent in educational ethnography are critical ethnography and auto-ethnography. The former approach is a theoretical and analytical form of ethnography with an emphasis on critically interpreting social structures and the role that human agency plays constructing the situations that people find themselves in (Aitkinson, Coffey, Delamont, Lofland & Lofland, 2001, p. 193; Fien & Hillcoat, 1996, pp. 35-36). As critical ethnography is influenced by Marxist and critical race theory, it also is driven to translate theoretical knowledge into social action (Madison, 2012, p. 16). The latter approach of auto-ethnography is a self conscious and introspective method of explaining cultural influences from the viewpoint of the researcher in connection to their wider social context (Ellis & Bochner, 2000, pp. 739-740). This approach often relies heavily on personal narratives since it is autobiographical by nature.

Role of the Researcher

The main objective of the ethnographer is to observe and record "naturally occurring behavior for retrospective reflection" through participant observation (Aubrey, 2000, p. 121). In order to become an insider in the community being studied, if the researcher is not already part of it, skills such as empathy, communication, awareness, and knowledge of typical behaviours need to be cultivated. In total, the ethnographer needs to be aware of the needs of both the individuals and community being studied, alongside the wider research community. Furthermore, since culture is such an integral part of ethnography, the ethnographer needs to reflect on their own conditioned cultural perspectives and how these influence and bias interactions and opinions with those who are being researched in order to avoid ethnocentrism.

Main Data Collecting Techniques

For ethnographic research an appropriate setting to perform a study will be the first requirement, including access into the community and permission from any necessary authoritative agencies (Aubrey, p. 122-123). From there, the ethnographer will need to decide on what role they will play in the community, alongside identifying whom and what will be specifically targeted for research. The methods used to collect raw data will include structured and non-structured interviews, note-taking, and questionnaires, with emphasis being placed on gathering first-hand information. Whilst there are numerous ways to collect data, these are some of the primary ones associated with fieldwork.

In terms of data analysis, the methods that are commonplace amongst ethnography include, inductive and recursive processes, construction of narratives, and applying "cultural and linguistic filters" to the information, such as ethnographic and conversation analysis (Li, 2009, p. 97). Inductive analysis involves examining the raw data for "thematic categorizations, inconsistencies, contradictions, to generate conclusions about what is happening and why" (Li, 2009, p. 100). Recursive analysis, which has parallels to the action research approach and is also referred to as "in the field analysis", is a process whereby there is a constant re-evaluation of hypotheses during fieldwork that reshapes data analysis into new and more relevant directions (LeCompte & Schensul, 2013, p. 27). Finally, the

6

construction of a narrative report will generally involve the description of the study, documentation of statistics, typical tendencies of the group and certain individuals, alongside a report of the more subjective accounts of behaviour, action, and observations noted by the ethnographer (Tomal, 2010, pp. 117-118). Throughout these methods the results may have been incorporated into some form of coding technique, such as grounded theory, which uses open, axial, or selective coding techniques to help categorize information and form propositions (Cottrell & Mckenzie, 2011, p. 233).

Critical Analysis

The strength of the ethnographic approach is that through understanding their own cultural perceptions, ethnographers are more likely to circumvent potential cultural barriers that may prevent them from gaining insider status, or at least, necessary information from being an accepted outsider (Aubrey, 2000, p. 118). Such barriers include ethnicity and the outward appearance of 'race', language barriers, and relevant power structure that are in place. In addition, ethnography is able to go beyond generalized "macro-theoretical explanations" of society through its in-depth analysis of "discrete social actions" (Pole & Marlene, 2003, p. 160). In doing so, it provides personalized accounts of social behaviour and issues from an insider's perspective, and then transcribes these into understandable structures and concepts that have a sound theoretical base.

The potential weaknesses arising during ethnography are that research participants may form a close or attached connection with the ethnographer, and then experience negative feelings at the conclusion of the research when the relationship ends, or perhaps they may be offended or hurt regarding how their thoughts or behaviors have been portrayed in the subsequent ethnography (Aitkinson et al, 2001, pp. 339-340). Furthermore, there is the possibility that those with power may use the research against those who have been studied. For example, when researching 'at risk' groups, such as the study of those who partake in unethical or illegal behaviours, there may be unknown negative ramifications. Another problem is that if the ethnographer is also the teacher unequal power differences need to be accounted for as well as responsibilities to the immediate function and needs of the classroom (Aubrey, 2000, p. 119). In addition, when dealing with minors, there is also the issue of gaining and perpetually re-visiting issues of informed consent. However, this matter is not specific to ethnography, but rather all types of research on minors.

Comparing Ethnography & Action Research

While both approaches have similarities in the fact that they are qualitative and share commonalities by way of potential data collection methods, the most prevalent differences are noted in three distinct areas: Aims, researcher status, and data analysis. The differences in the aims are highlighted between the intention of the action researcher (ARer) in gaining knowledge for the primary reason of implementing practical changes in their environment setting, compared to the ethnographer's goal to advance theoretical knowledge in the immediate area and wider academic arena (Punch, 2009, pp. 127-136). While the ethnographer may also have a desire to concretely help those in the community being studied, this may not necessarily translate to practice. The difference between the two approaches is illustrated by the fact that the ARer has a more vested interest in practically changing their own educational environment than the ethnographer, who is typically not part of the group they are researching and may only be interested in furthering academic knowledge. The significance of this is that the ARer will have a more active role within the community or learning institute, as well as a stronger interest in seeing through any potential changes. There are, however, closer similarities between AR and those applying critical ethnography, with the latter having close ties to creating social change (Madison, 2012, p. 16).

The differences surrounding researcher status are primarily focused around the position the researcher has within the group being studied. In AR, the researcher is typically an insider who intimately knows those involved (Sheehy, 2005, p. 205). Furthermore, the ARer is also a key actor within the research, directing with action and intention. In contrast, the ethnographer is usually an outsider, who has gained access to the educational setting (Aubrey, 2000, p. 121). The role they take may be participant observation; however, it can also be non-participant observation, rendering a passive role in contrast to the ARer. Finally, the differences surrounding data analysis revolve around when it is completed (Punch, 2009, pp. 124-137). In AR, there is a constant analysis throughout the study, as the cyclical method demands. In ethnography, the analysis is normally done at the conclusion of the fieldwork. Additionally, the time spend in the field collecting the data will be more prolonged in an ethnographic study, as there needs to be a period where the researcher can gain close enough access to those involved. The methods involved in data analysis also can differ between AR and ethnography, though this will usually depend more on the researcher's own theoretical stance rather than if they follow an orthodox AR or ethnographic approach, especially since a mixed-methods approach is common within qualitative research (Punch, 2209, pp. 169-203).

In conclusion, AR and ethnography are both valuable tools for any researcher looking to analyze and interpret conditions in the educational sector. While they both have their notable strengths and limitations, it should be noted that neither approach is incompatible with the other and elements from either approach can be utilised to complement other qualitative techniques. In the end, whether one decides to use AR, ethnography, or a fusion of both, will depend on their practical and theoretical position coming into the study.

References

Atkins, L., & Wallace, S. (2012). *Qualitative research in education*. Thousand Oaks, CA: Sage Publications.

Atkinson, P., Coffey, A., Delamont, S., Lofland, J., & Lofland, L. (2001). *Handbook of ethnography*. London, U.K: Sage Publications.

Aubrey, C. (2000). *Early childhood educational research: Issues in methodology and ethics*. London, U.K: Falmer Press.

Bassey, M. (1998). Action research for improving educational practice. In R. Halsall (Eds.), *Teacher research and school improvement: Opening doors from the inside* (pp. 94-95). Buckingham, UK: Open University Press.

Cohen, L., Manion, L., & Morrison, K. (2007). *Research methods in education* (6th ed.). London, UK: Routledge.

Cottrell, R., & Mckenzie, J. (2011). *Health promotion and education research methods: Using the five chapter thesis/dissertation model*. Sudbury, MA: Jones and Bartlett Publishers.

Costello, P. M. (2011). *Effective action research: Developing reflective thinking and practice* (2nd ed.). London, UK: Continuum.

Craig, D. (2009). *Action research essentials*. San Francisco, CA: Jossey-Bass.

Ellis, C., & Bochner, A. (2000). Autoethnography, personal narrative, and personal reflexivity. In N. Denzin & Y. Lincoln (Eds.), *Handbook of qualitative research* (2nd ed., pp. 733-763). Thousand Oaks, CA: Sage Publications.

Eller, J. (2009). *Cultural anthropology: Global forces, local lives*. New York, NY: Routledge.

Fien, J., & Hillcoat, J. (1996). The critical tradition in research in geographical and environmental education research. In M. Williams (Eds.), *Understanding geographical and environmental education: The role of research* (pp. 26-40). London, U.K: Cassell.

Haviland.W., Prins. H., McBride.B., & Walrath, D. (2011). *Cultural anthropology: The human challenge* (13th ed.). Belmont, CA: Wadsworth.

Kemmis, S., & Mctaggart, R. (2000). Participatory action research. In N. Denzin & Y. Lincoln (Eds.), *Handbook of qualitative research* (2nd ed., pp. 567-605). Thousand Oaks, CA: Sage Publications.

LeCompte, M., & Schensul, J. (2013). *Analysis & interpretation of ethnographic data: A mixed methods approach* (2nd ed.). Plymouth, U.K: AltaMira Press.

Li, Y. (2009). *Classroom culture and the construction of learning opportunities: An ethnographic case study of two EFL classrooms in a higher education setting in China*. Taipei, Taiwan: Showwe Information Co.

Madison, S. (2012). *Critical ethnography: Method, ethics, and performance* (2nd Ed.). Thousand Oaks: CA: Sage Publications.

Manfra, M. (2009). Action research: Exploring the theoretical divide between practical and clinical approaches. *Journal of Curriculum and Instruction, 3*(1), 32-46.

Mertler, C. (2006). *Action research: Teachers as researchers in the classroom.* Thousand Oaks, CA: Sage Publications.

Motley-Abbott, R. M. (2007). Transformative learning in nonformal education: An action research study examining epistemological differences among women in an addiction recovery support program. *Dissertation Abstracts International Section A, 67.*

Parsons, R., & Brown, K. (2002). *Teacher as reflective practitioner and action researcher.* Belmont, CA: Wadsworth.

Pole, C., & Marlene, M. (2003). *Ethnography for education.* Berkshire, U.K: Open University Press.

Punch, K. (2009). *Introduction to research methods in education.* Los Angeles, CA: Sage Publications.

Spindler, G., & Hammond, L. (2006). *Innovations in educational ethnography: Theory, methods, and results.* Mahwah, N.J: Lawrence Erlbaum Associates.

Tomal, D. (2010). *Action research for educators* (2nd Ed.). Plymouth, U.K: Rowman & Littlefield Publishers.

Waters-Adam (2006). *Action research in education.* Retrieved from http://www.edu.plymouth.ac.uk/resined/actionresearch/arhome.htm

Whyte, W.F. (1989). Advancing scientific knowledge through participatory action research. *Sociological Forum, 4*(3), 367-385.

Zeni, J. (2005). A guide to ethical issues and action research. In K. Sheehy. ,M. Nind., J. Rix & K. Simmons (Eds.), *Ethics and research in inclusive education: Values into practice* (pp. 205-214). New York, NY: RoutledgeFalmer.